D1106107

READING POWER

In the Ring with Scott Steiner

Michael Payan

The Rosen Publishing Group's
PowerKids Press ™
New York

To Mom and Dad...you are the strength in my life...thank you

Published in 2002 by The Rosen Publishing Group, Inc.
29 East 21st Street, New York, NY 10010

First Edition

Book Design: Michael Donnellan

Photo Credits: All photos by Colin Bowman.

Payan, Michael.
In the ring with Scott Steiner / Michael Payan.
    p. cm. — (Wrestlers)
Includes bibliographical references (p.) and index.
ISBN 0-8239-6043-9
1. Steiner, Scott—Juvenile literature. 2. Wrestlers—United
States—Biography—Juvenile literature. [1. Steiner, Scott. 2. Wrestlers.] I. Title.
GV1196.S743 P39 2002
796.812'092—dc21

                                                            00-013204

Manufactured in the United States of America

Contents

Scott Steiner is a wrestler.
He is very strong.

5

Scott has big muscles.

Scott wears a belt. He won this belt in a match.

Scott is in the air. Scott knocks down Booker T.

13

Scott is upside down. He holds Booker T's head between his knees.

15

Scott is strong. He can catch people in the air.

Scott kisses his big muscles. He is proud of his big muscles.

Scott wears sunglasses.
Scott looks cool.

Glossary

belt (BEHLT) What a wrestler gets for winning a match.

muscles (MUH-suhlz) Parts of the body underneath the skin that can be tightened or loosened to make the body move.

proud (PROWD) Having or showing a lot of confidence in yourself.

Here are more books to read about wrestling:

Slammin': Wrestling's Greatest Heroes and Villains
by David Hofstede
E C W Press (1999)

Wrestling Renegades: An In-Depth Look at Today's Superstars of Pro Wrestling
By Daniel Cohen
Archway (1999)

To learn more about Scott Steiner, check out this Web site:

www.wcw.com/2000/superstars/scott.steiner/

Index

Word Count: 78

Note to Librarians, Teachers, and Parents

If reading is a challenge, Reading Power is a solution! Reading Power is perfect for readers who want high-interest subject matter at an accessible reading level. These fact-filled, photo-illustrated books are designed for readers who want straightforward vocabulary, engaging topics, and a manageable reading experience. With clear picture/text correspondence, leveled Reading Power books put the reader in charge. Now readers have the power to get the information they want and the skills they need in a user-friendly format.